SERMON NOTES FOR KIDS

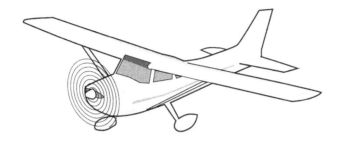

this belongs to

_____

DATE: / /

WHO IS SPEAKING?

FAVORITE SONG THAT WAS SUNG TODAY:

DRAW SOMETHING FROM TODAY'S BIBLE STORY

WHAT WAS THE SERMON ABOUT?

SOMETHING I'D LIKE TO PRAY FOR:

WORDS I HEARD BUT DIDN'T UNDERSTAND:

ONE THING GOD'S WORD TAUGHT ME TODAY:

A DECISION I MADE FOR THE LORD:

QUESTIONS I HAVE:

DATE: / /

WHO IS SPEAKING?

FAVORITE SONG THAT WAS SUNG TODAY:

DRAW SOMETHING FROM TODAY'S BIBLE STORY

WHAT WAS THE SERMON ABOUT?

SOMETHING I'D LIKE TO PRAY FOR:

WORDS I HEARD BUT DIDN'T UNDERSTAND:

ONE THING GOD'S WORD TAUGHT ME TODAY:

A DECISION I MADE FOR THE LORD:

QUESTIONS I HAVE:

DATE: / /

FAVORITE SONG THAT WAS SUNG TODAY:

WHO IS SPEAKING?

DRAW SOMETHING FROM TODAY'S BIBLE STORY

WHAT WAS THE SERMON ABOUT?

SOMETHING I'D LIKE TO PRAY FOR:

WORDS I HEARD BUT DIDN'T UNDERSTAND:

ONE THING GOD'S WORD TAUGHT ME TODAY:

A DECISION I MADE FOR THE LORD:

QUESTIONS I HAVE:

DATE: / /

WHO IS SPEAKING?

FAVORITE SONG THAT WAS SUNG TODAY:

DRAW SOMETHING FROM TODAY'S BIBLE STORY

WHAT WAS THE SERMON ABOUT?

SOMETHING I'D LIKE TO PRAY FOR:

WORDS I HEARD BUT DIDN'T UNDERSTAND:

ONE THING GOD'S WORD TAUGHT ME TODAY:

A DECISION I MADE FOR THE LORD:

QUESTIONS I HAVE:

DATE: / /

WHO IS SPEAKING?

FAVORITE SONG THAT WAS SUNG TODAY:

DRAW SOMETHING FROM TODAY'S BIBLE STORY

WHAT WAS THE SERMON ABOUT?

SOMETHING I'D LIKE TO PRAY FOR:

WORDS I HEARD BUT DIDN'T UNDERSTAND:

ONE THING GOD'S WORD TAUGHT ME TODAY:

A DECISION I MADE FOR THE LORD:

QUESTIONS I HAVE:

DATE: / /

WHO IS SPEAKING?

FAVORITE SONG THAT
WAS SUNG TODAY:

DRAW SOMETHING FROM TODAY'S BIBLE STORY

WHAT WAS THE SERMON ABOUT?

SOMETHING I'D LIKE TO PRAY FOR:

WORDS I HEARD BUT DIDN'T UNDERSTAND:

ONE THING GOD'S WORD TAUGHT ME TODAY:

A DECISION I MADE FOR THE LORD:

QUESTIONS I HAVE:

WHO IS SPEAKING?

DATE: / /

FAVORITE SONG THAT WAS SUNG TODAY:

DRAW SOMETHING FROM TODAY'S BIBLE STORY

WHAT WAS THE SERMON ABOUT?

SOMETHING I'D LIKE TO PRAY FOR:

WORDS I HEARD BUT DIDN'T UNDERSTAND:

ONE THING GOD'S WORD TAUGHT ME TODAY:

A DECISION I MADE FOR THE LORD:

QUESTIONS I HAVE:

DATE: / /

WHO IS SPEAKING?

FAVORITE SONG THAT
WAS SUNG TODAY:

DRAW SOMETHING FROM TODAY'S BIBLE STORY

WHAT WAS THE SERMON ABOUT?

SOMETHING I'D LIKE TO PRAY FOR:

WORDS I HEARD BUT DIDN'T UNDERSTAND:

ONE THING GOD'S WORD TAUGHT ME TODAY:

A DECISION I MADE FOR THE LORD:

QUESTIONS I HAVE:

DATE: / /

WHO IS SPEAKING?

FAVORITE SONG THAT
WAS SUNG TODAY:

DRAW SOMETHING FROM TODAY'S BIBLE STORY

WHAT WAS THE SERMON ABOUT?

SOMETHING I'D LIKE TO PRAY FOR:

WORDS I HEARD BUT DIDN'T UNDERSTAND:

ONE THING GOD'S WORD TAUGHT ME TODAY:

A DECISION I MADE FOR THE LORD:

QUESTIONS I HAVE:

DATE: / /

WHO IS SPEAKING?

FAVORITE SONG THAT WAS SUNG TODAY:

DRAW SOMETHING FROM TODAY'S BIBLE STORY

WHAT WAS THE SERMON ABOUT?

SOMETHING I'D LIKE TO PRAY FOR:

WORDS I HEARD BUT DIDN'T UNDERSTAND:

ONE THING GOD'S WORD TAUGHT ME TODAY:

A DECISION I MADE FOR THE LORD:

QUESTIONS I HAVE:

DATE: / /

WHO IS SPEAKING?

FAVORITE SONG THAT WAS SUNG TODAY:

DRAW SOMETHING FROM TODAY'S BIBLE STORY

WHAT WAS THE SERMON ABOUT?

SOMETHING I'D LIKE TO PRAY FOR:

WORDS I HEARD BUT DIDN'T UNDERSTAND:

ONE THING GOD'S WORD TAUGHT ME TODAY:

A DECISION I MADE FOR THE LORD:

QUESTIONS I HAVE:

DATE: ___ / ___ / ___

WHO IS SPEAKING?

FAVORITE SONG THAT WAS SUNG TODAY:

DRAW SOMETHING FROM TODAY'S BIBLE STORY

WHAT WAS THE SERMON ABOUT?

SOMETHING I'D LIKE TO PRAY FOR:

WORDS I HEARD BUT DIDN'T UNDERSTAND:

ONE THING GOD'S WORD TAUGHT ME TODAY:

A DECISION I MADE FOR THE LORD:

QUESTIONS I HAVE:

DATE: / /

WHO IS SPEAKING?

FAVORITE SONG THAT WAS SUNG TODAY:

DRAW SOMETHING FROM TODAY'S BIBLE STORY

WHAT WAS THE SERMON ABOUT?

SOMETHING I'D LIKE TO PRAY FOR:

WORDS I HEARD BUT DIDN'T UNDERSTAND:

ONE THING GOD'S WORD TAUGHT ME TODAY:

A DECISION I MADE FOR THE LORD:

QUESTIONS I HAVE:

DATE: / /

WHO IS SPEAKING?

FAVORITE SONG THAT WAS SUNG TODAY:

DRAW SOMETHING FROM TODAY'S BIBLE STORY

WHAT WAS THE SERMON ABOUT?

SOMETHING I'D LIKE TO PRAY FOR:

WORDS I HEARD BUT DIDN'T UNDERSTAND:

ONE THING GOD'S WORD TAUGHT ME TODAY:

A DECISION I MADE FOR THE LORD:

QUESTIONS I HAVE:

DATE: / /

WHO IS SPEAKING?

FAVORITE SONG THAT WAS SUNG TODAY:

DRAW SOMETHING FROM TODAY'S BIBLE STORY

WHAT WAS THE SERMON ABOUT?

SOMETHING I'D LIKE TO PRAY FOR:

WORDS I HEARD BUT DIDN'T UNDERSTAND:

ONE THING GOD'S WORD TAUGHT ME TODAY:

A DECISION I MADE FOR THE LORD:

QUESTIONS I HAVE:

DATE: / /

WHO IS SPEAKING?

FAVORITE SONG THAT WAS SUNG TODAY:

DRAW SOMETHING FROM TODAY'S BIBLE STORY

WHAT WAS THE SERMON ABOUT?

SOMETHING I'D LIKE TO PRAY FOR:

WORDS I HEARD BUT DIDN'T UNDERSTAND:

ONE THING GOD'S WORD TAUGHT ME TODAY:

A DECISION I MADE FOR THE LORD:

QUESTIONS I HAVE:

DATE: / /

WHO IS SPEAKING?

FAVORITE SONG THAT WAS SUNG TODAY:

DRAW SOMETHING FROM TODAY'S BIBLE STORY

WHAT WAS THE SERMON ABOUT?

SOMETHING I'D LIKE TO PRAY FOR:

WORDS I HEARD BUT DIDN'T UNDERSTAND:

ONE THING GOD'S WORD TAUGHT ME TODAY:

A DECISION I MADE FOR THE LORD:

QUESTIONS I HAVE:

DATE: / /

WHO IS SPEAKING?

FAVORITE SONG THAT WAS SUNG TODAY:

DRAW SOMETHING FROM TODAY'S BIBLE STORY

WHAT WAS THE SERMON ABOUT?

SOMETHING I'D LIKE TO PRAY FOR:

WORDS I HEARD BUT DIDN'T UNDERSTAND:

ONE THING GOD'S WORD TAUGHT ME TODAY:

A DECISION I MADE FOR THE LORD:

QUESTIONS I HAVE:

DATE: / /

WHO IS SPEAKING?

FAVORITE SONG THAT
WAS SUNG TODAY:

DRAW SOMETHING FROM TODAY'S BIBLE STORY

WHAT WAS THE SERMON ABOUT?

SOMETHING I'D LIKE TO PRAY FOR:

WORDS I HEARD BUT DIDN'T UNDERSTAND:

ONE THING GOD'S WORD TAUGHT ME TODAY:

A DECISION I MADE FOR THE LORD:

QUESTIONS I HAVE:

DATE: / /

WHO IS SPEAKING?

FAVORITE SONG THAT WAS SUNG TODAY:

DRAW SOMETHING FROM TODAY'S BIBLE STORY

WHAT WAS THE SERMON ABOUT?

SOMETHING I'D LIKE TO PRAY FOR:

WORDS I HEARD BUT DIDN'T UNDERSTAND:

ONE THING GOD'S WORD TAUGHT ME TODAY:

A DECISION I MADE FOR THE LORD:

QUESTIONS I HAVE:

DATE: / /

WHO IS SPEAKING?

FAVORITE SONG THAT WAS SUNG TODAY:

DRAW SOMETHING FROM TODAY'S BIBLE STORY

WHAT WAS THE SERMON ABOUT?

SOMETHING I'D LIKE TO PRAY FOR:

WORDS I HEARD BUT DIDN'T UNDERSTAND:

ONE THING GOD'S WORD TAUGHT ME TODAY:

A DECISION I MADE FOR THE LORD:

QUESTIONS I HAVE:

DATE: / /

WHO IS SPEAKING?

FAVORITE SONG THAT WAS SUNG TODAY:

DRAW SOMETHING FROM TODAY'S BIBLE STORY

WHAT WAS THE SERMON ABOUT?

SOMETHING I'D LIKE TO PRAY FOR:

WORDS I HEARD BUT DIDN'T UNDERSTAND:

ONE THING GOD'S WORD TAUGHT ME TODAY:

A DECISION I MADE FOR THE LORD:

QUESTIONS I HAVE:

DATE: / /

WHO IS SPEAKING?

FAVORITE SONG THAT WAS SUNG TODAY:

DRAW SOMETHING FROM TODAY'S BIBLE STORY

WHAT WAS THE SERMON ABOUT?

SOMETHING I'D LIKE TO PRAY FOR:

WORDS I HEARD BUT DIDN'T UNDERSTAND:

ONE THING GOD'S WORD TAUGHT ME TODAY:

A DECISION I MADE FOR THE LORD:

QUESTIONS I HAVE:

DATE: / /

WHO IS SPEAKING?

FAVORITE SONG THAT WAS SUNG TODAY:

DRAW SOMETHING FROM TODAY'S BIBLE STORY

WHAT WAS THE SERMON ABOUT?

SOMETHING I'D LIKE TO PRAY FOR:

WORDS I HEARD BUT DIDN'T UNDERSTAND:

ONE THING GOD'S WORD TAUGHT ME TODAY:

A DECISION I MADE FOR THE LORD:

QUESTIONS I HAVE:

DATE: / /

WHO IS SPEAKING?

FAVORITE SONG THAT WAS SUNG TODAY:

DRAW SOMETHING FROM TODAY'S BIBLE STORY

WHAT WAS THE SERMON ABOUT?

SOMETHING I'D LIKE TO PRAY FOR:

WORDS I HEARD BUT DIDN'T UNDERSTAND:

ONE THING GOD'S WORD TAUGHT ME TODAY:

A DECISION I MADE FOR THE LORD:

QUESTIONS I HAVE:

DATE: / /

WHO IS SPEAKING?

FAVORITE SONG THAT
WAS SUNG TODAY:

DRAW SOMETHING FROM TODAY'S BIBLE STORY

WHAT WAS THE SERMON ABOUT?

SOMETHING I'D LIKE TO PRAY FOR:

WORDS I HEARD BUT DIDN'T UNDERSTAND:

ONE THING GOD'S WORD TAUGHT ME TODAY:

A DECISION I MADE FOR THE LORD:

QUESTIONS I HAVE:

DATE: ___ / ___ / ___

WHO IS SPEAKING?

FAVORITE SONG THAT WAS SUNG TODAY:

DRAW SOMETHING FROM TODAY'S BIBLE STORY

WHAT WAS THE SERMON ABOUT?

SOMETHING I'D LIKE TO PRAY FOR:

WORDS I HEARD BUT DIDN'T UNDERSTAND:

ONE THING GOD'S WORD TAUGHT ME TODAY:

A DECISION I MADE FOR THE LORD:

QUESTIONS I HAVE:

DATE: / /

WHO IS SPEAKING?

FAVORITE SONG THAT WAS SUNG TODAY:

DRAW SOMETHING FROM TODAY'S BIBLE STORY

WHAT WAS THE SERMON ABOUT?

SOMETHING I'D LIKE TO PRAY FOR:

WORDS I HEARD BUT DIDN'T UNDERSTAND:

ONE THING GOD'S WORD TAUGHT ME TODAY:

A DECISION I MADE FOR THE LORD:

QUESTIONS I HAVE:

DATE: / /

WHO IS SPEAKING?

FAVORITE SONG THAT WAS SUNG TODAY:

DRAW SOMETHING FROM TODAY'S BIBLE STORY

WHAT WAS THE SERMON ABOUT?

SOMETHING I'D LIKE TO PRAY FOR:

WORDS I HEARD BUT DIDN'T UNDERSTAND:

ONE THING GOD'S WORD TAUGHT ME TODAY:

A DECISION I MADE FOR THE LORD:

QUESTIONS I HAVE:

DATE: / /

WHO IS SPEAKING?

FAVORITE SONG THAT WAS SUNG TODAY:

DRAW SOMETHING FROM TODAY'S BIBLE STORY

WHAT WAS THE SERMON ABOUT?

SOMETHING I'D LIKE TO PRAY FOR:

WORDS I HEARD BUT DIDN'T UNDERSTAND:

ONE THING GOD'S WORD TAUGHT ME TODAY:

A DECISION I MADE FOR THE LORD:

QUESTIONS I HAVE:

DATE: / /

WHO IS SPEAKING?

FAVORITE SONG THAT WAS SUNG TODAY:

DRAW SOMETHING FROM TODAY'S BIBLE STORY

WHAT WAS THE SERMON ABOUT?

SOMETHING I'D LIKE TO PRAY FOR:

WORDS I HEARD BUT DIDN'T UNDERSTAND:

ONE THING GOD'S WORD TAUGHT ME TODAY:

A DECISION I MADE FOR THE LORD:

QUESTIONS I HAVE:

DATE: / /

WHO IS SPEAKING?

FAVORITE SONG THAT WAS SUNG TODAY:

DRAW SOMETHING FROM TODAY'S BIBLE STORY

WHAT WAS THE SERMON ABOUT?

SOMETHING I'D LIKE TO PRAY FOR:

WORDS I HEARD BUT DIDN'T UNDERSTAND:

ONE THING GOD'S WORD TAUGHT ME TODAY:

A DECISION I MADE FOR THE LORD:

QUESTIONS I HAVE:

DATE: / /

FAVORITE SONG THAT WAS SUNG TODAY:

WHO IS SPEAKING?

DRAW SOMETHING FROM TODAY'S BIBLE STORY

WHAT WAS THE SERMON ABOUT?

SOMETHING I'D LIKE TO PRAY FOR:

WORDS I HEARD BUT DIDN'T UNDERSTAND:

ONE THING GOD'S WORD TAUGHT ME TODAY:

A DECISION I MADE FOR THE LORD:

QUESTIONS I HAVE:

DATE: / /

WHO IS SPEAKING?

FAVORITE SONG THAT WAS SUNG TODAY:

DRAW SOMETHING FROM TODAY'S BIBLE STORY

WHAT WAS THE SERMON ABOUT?

SOMETHING I'D LIKE TO PRAY FOR:

WORDS I HEARD BUT DIDN'T UNDERSTAND:

ONE THING GOD'S WORD TAUGHT ME TODAY:

A DECISION I MADE FOR THE LORD:

QUESTIONS I HAVE:

DATE: / /

WHO IS SPEAKING?

FAVORITE SONG THAT WAS SUNG TODAY:

DRAW SOMETHING FROM TODAY'S BIBLE STORY

WHAT WAS THE SERMON ABOUT?

SOMETHING I'D LIKE TO PRAY FOR:

WORDS I HEARD BUT DIDN'T UNDERSTAND:

ONE THING GOD'S WORD TAUGHT ME TODAY:

A DECISION I MADE FOR THE LORD:

QUESTIONS I HAVE:

DATE: /   /

WHO IS SPEAKING?

FAVORITE SONG THAT WAS SUNG TODAY:

DRAW SOMETHING FROM TODAY'S BIBLE STORY

WHAT WAS THE SERMON ABOUT?

SOMETHING I'D LIKE TO PRAY FOR:

WORDS I HEARD BUT DIDN'T UNDERSTAND:

ONE THING GOD'S WORD TAUGHT ME TODAY:

A DECISION I MADE FOR THE LORD:

QUESTIONS I HAVE:

DATE: / /

FAVORITE SONG THAT WAS SUNG TODAY:

WHO IS SPEAKING?

DRAW SOMETHING FROM TODAY'S BIBLE STORY

WHAT WAS THE SERMON ABOUT?

SOMETHING I'D LIKE TO PRAY FOR:

WORDS I HEARD BUT DIDN'T UNDERSTAND:

ONE THING GOD'S WORD TAUGHT ME TODAY:

A DECISION I MADE FOR THE LORD:

QUESTIONS I HAVE:

DATE: / /

WHO IS SPEAKING?

FAVORITE SONG THAT
WAS SUNG TODAY:

DRAW SOMETHING FROM TODAY'S BIBLE STORY

WHAT WAS THE SERMON ABOUT?

SOMETHING I'D LIKE TO PRAY FOR:

WORDS I HEARD BUT DIDN'T UNDERSTAND:

ONE THING GOD'S WORD TAUGHT ME TODAY:

A DECISION I MADE FOR THE LORD:

QUESTIONS I HAVE:

DATE: / /

WHO IS SPEAKING?

FAVORITE SONG THAT WAS SUNG TODAY:

DRAW SOMETHING FROM TODAY'S BIBLE STORY

WHAT WAS THE SERMON ABOUT?

SOMETHING I'D LIKE TO PRAY FOR:

WORDS I HEARD BUT DIDN'T UNDERSTAND:

ONE THING GOD'S WORD TAUGHT ME TODAY:

A DECISION I MADE FOR THE LORD:

QUESTIONS I HAVE:

DATE: / /

WHO IS SPEAKING?

FAVORITE SONG THAT WAS SUNG TODAY:

DRAW SOMETHING FROM TODAY'S BIBLE STORY

WHAT WAS THE SERMON ABOUT?

SOMETHING I'D LIKE TO PRAY FOR:

WORDS I HEARD BUT DIDN'T UNDERSTAND:

ONE THING GOD'S WORD TAUGHT ME TODAY:

A DECISION I MADE FOR THE LORD:

QUESTIONS I HAVE:

DATE: / /

WHO IS SPEAKING?

FAVORITE SONG THAT WAS SUNG TODAY:

DRAW SOMETHING FROM TODAY'S BIBLE STORY

WHAT WAS THE SERMON ABOUT?

SOMETHING I'D LIKE TO PRAY FOR:

WORDS I HEARD BUT DIDN'T UNDERSTAND:

ONE THING GOD'S WORD TAUGHT ME TODAY:

A DECISION I MADE FOR THE LORD:

QUESTIONS I HAVE:

DATE: / /

WHO IS SPEAKING?

FAVORITE SONG THAT
WAS SUNG TODAY:

DRAW SOMETHING FROM TODAY'S BIBLE STORY

WHAT WAS THE SERMON ABOUT?

SOMETHING I'D LIKE TO PRAY FOR:

WORDS I HEARD BUT DIDN'T UNDERSTAND:

ONE THING GOD'S WORD TAUGHT ME TODAY:

A DECISION I MADE FOR THE LORD:

QUESTIONS I HAVE:

DATE: / /

WHO IS SPEAKING?

FAVORITE SONG THAT WAS SUNG TODAY:

DRAW SOMETHING FROM TODAY'S BIBLE STORY

WHAT WAS THE SERMON ABOUT?

SOMETHING I'D LIKE TO PRAY FOR:

WORDS I HEARD BUT DIDN'T UNDERSTAND:

ONE THING GOD'S WORD TAUGHT ME TODAY:

A DECISION I MADE FOR THE LORD:

QUESTIONS I HAVE:

DATE: / /

WHO IS SPEAKING?

FAVORITE SONG THAT WAS SUNG TODAY:

DRAW SOMETHING FROM TODAY'S BIBLE STORY

WHAT WAS THE SERMON ABOUT?

SOMETHING I'D LIKE TO PRAY FOR:

WORDS I HEARD BUT DIDN'T UNDERSTAND:

ONE THING GOD'S WORD TAUGHT ME TODAY:

A DECISION I MADE FOR THE LORD:

QUESTIONS I HAVE:

DATE: / /

WHO IS SPEAKING?

FAVORITE SONG THAT WAS SUNG TODAY:

DRAW SOMETHING FROM TODAY'S BIBLE STORY

WHAT WAS THE SERMON ABOUT?

SOMETHING I'D LIKE TO PRAY FOR:

WORDS I HEARD BUT DIDN'T UNDERSTAND:

ONE THING GOD'S WORD TAUGHT ME TODAY:

A DECISION I MADE FOR THE LORD:

QUESTIONS I HAVE:

DATE: / /

WHO IS SPEAKING?

FAVORITE SONG THAT WAS SUNG TODAY:

DRAW SOMETHING FROM TODAY'S BIBLE STORY

WHAT WAS THE SERMON ABOUT?

SOMETHING I'D LIKE TO PRAY FOR:

WORDS I HEARD BUT DIDN'T UNDERSTAND:

ONE THING GOD'S WORD TAUGHT ME TODAY:

A DECISION I MADE FOR THE LORD:

QUESTIONS I HAVE:

DATE: / /

WHO IS SPEAKING?

FAVORITE SONG THAT WAS SUNG TODAY:

DRAW SOMETHING FROM TODAY'S BIBLE STORY

WHAT WAS THE SERMON ABOUT?

SOMETHING I'D LIKE TO PRAY FOR:

WORDS I HEARD BUT DIDN'T UNDERSTAND:

ONE THING GOD'S WORD TAUGHT ME TODAY:

A DECISION I MADE FOR THE LORD:

QUESTIONS I HAVE:

DATE: / /

WHO IS SPEAKING?

FAVORITE SONG THAT
WAS SUNG TODAY:

DRAW SOMETHING FROM TODAY'S BIBLE STORY

WHAT WAS THE SERMON ABOUT?

SOMETHING I'D LIKE TO PRAY FOR:

WORDS I HEARD BUT DIDN'T UNDERSTAND:

ONE THING GOD'S WORD TAUGHT ME TODAY:

A DECISION I MADE FOR THE LORD:

QUESTIONS I HAVE:

DATE: / /

WHO IS SPEAKING?

FAVORITE SONG THAT WAS SUNG TODAY:

DRAW SOMETHING FROM TODAY'S BIBLE STORY

WHAT WAS THE SERMON ABOUT?

SOMETHING I'D LIKE TO PRAY FOR:

WORDS I HEARD BUT DIDN'T UNDERSTAND:

ONE THING GOD'S WORD TAUGHT ME TODAY:

A DECISION I MADE FOR THE LORD:

QUESTIONS I HAVE:

DATE: / /

WHO IS SPEAKING?

FAVORITE SONG THAT WAS SUNG TODAY:

DRAW SOMETHING FROM TODAY'S BIBLE STORY

WHAT WAS THE SERMON ABOUT?

SOMETHING I'D LIKE TO PRAY FOR:

WORDS I HEARD BUT DIDN'T UNDERSTAND:

ONE THING GOD'S WORD TAUGHT ME TODAY:

A DECISION I MADE FOR THE LORD:

QUESTIONS I HAVE:

DATE: / /

WHO IS SPEAKING?

FAVORITE SONG THAT WAS SUNG TODAY:

DRAW SOMETHING FROM TODAY'S BIBLE STORY

WHAT WAS THE SERMON ABOUT?

SOMETHING I'D LIKE TO PRAY FOR:

WORDS I HEARD BUT DIDN'T UNDERSTAND:

ONE THING GOD'S WORD TAUGHT ME TODAY:

A DECISION I MADE FOR THE LORD:

QUESTIONS I HAVE:

DATE: / /

WHO IS SPEAKING?

FAVORITE SONG THAT WAS SUNG TODAY:

DRAW SOMETHING FROM TODAY'S BIBLE STORY

WHAT WAS THE SERMON ABOUT?

SOMETHING I'D LIKE TO PRAY FOR:

WORDS I HEARD BUT DIDN'T UNDERSTAND:

ONE THING GOD'S WORD TAUGHT ME TODAY:

A DECISION I MADE FOR THE LORD:

QUESTIONS I HAVE:

To order more copies and to see a variety of styles
available go to Amazon.com and search for
Family Closet Treasures Sermon Notes

CPSIA information can be obtained
at www.ICGtesting.com
Printed in the USA
LVHW031213211019
634829LV00008B/3200/P